Generation Next, by Michael Bradley

A Sports Illustrated For Kids publication/July 2004

Sports Illustrated For Kids and are registered trademarks of Time Inc.

Cover and interior design by Edward Duarte
Front-cover photos: Peyton Manning by Bob Rosato/Sports Illustrated; Archie Manning by John Iacono/Sports Illustrated; Patrick Ewing by Manny Millan/Sports Illustrated; Patrick Ewing, Jr., by AJ Mast/Icon SMI
Back-cover photos: Prince Fielder by J2 Photographic; Cecil Fielder by Damian Strohmeyer/Sports Illustrated

For information, address: Sports Illustrated For Kids

ISBN: 1-930623-33-X

Generation Next is published by Sports Illustrated For Kids, a division of Time Inc. Its trademark is registered in the U.S. Patent and Trademark Office and in other countries. Sports Illustrated For Kids, 135 W. 50th Street, New York, NY 10020-1393.

PRINTED IN THE UNITED STATES

10 9 8 7 6 5 4 3 2 1

Generation Next is a production of Sports Illustrated For Kids and Sports Illustrated For Kids Books: Erin Egan, Senior Editor/Editorial Projects; Ron Berler, Project Editor; Edward Duarte, Designer; Greg Payan, Photo Editor; Stephen Caruso, Thaddeus Hartmann, Lindsey Reu, Reporters; Timothy E. Pitt, Director of Editorial Operations; Steve Chanin, Page Makeup Deputy; Marilyn Goldman, Production Manager

Sports Illustrated **KIDS**
SPECIAL EDITION

Peyton Manning

Archie Manning

Generation
NEXT
SUPERSTAR ATHLETES
WITH SUPERSTAR DADS

Patrick Ewing, Jr.

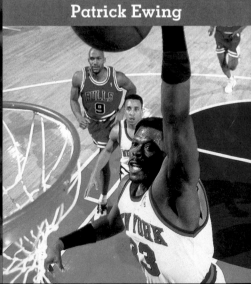
Patrick Ewing

Generation NEXT

Fernando
Valenzuela,
Sr. and Jr.

Karl Malone
and Cheryl
Ford

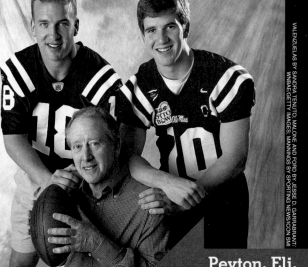

Peyton, Eli,
and Archie
Manning

CONTEN

TS

Sean Burroughs plays third base for the San Diego Padres. To find out who his famous dad is, turn to page 22.

Peyton and Eli MANNING

Quarterback Peyton Manning of the Indianapolis Colts finished the 2003 season with 29 touchdowns and 4,267 passing yards. It was the fifth straight season he had passed for at least 4,000 yards. At Tennessee, he set 33 school records and was a three-time Academic All-America.

Manning's dad, Archie, was a star quarterback at Mississippi who played mainly for the New Orleans Saints. He had 4,753 passing yards in college and 23,911 in the NFL. Peyton had 11,201 yards in college and 24,885 yards in the NFL at the start of the 2004 season.

But another Manning just might match Peyton's numbers someday. His younger brother, Eli, is the New York Giants' rookie quarterback. He set or tied 47 school records in four seasons at Mississippi, including most passing yards (10,119) and most touchdown passes (81).

Peyton and Eli are classic, drop-back passers with strong, accurate arms and the smarts to pick apart an opponent's defense. "There's a lot of similarities between Peyton and me," Eli told S.I. FOR KIDS. "We both have quick releases and keep the ball up high. Neither of us is extremely fast. We try to have the mental part of the game down to get an advantage."

Now that both brothers are in the NFL, let the comparisons begin.

■ About Peyton

Height: 6' 5"   Weight: 230 lbs.

Birth Date: March 24, 1976

Birthplace: New Orleans, Louisiana

Team/Position: Indianapolis Colts/Quarterback

Accomplishments:

- Four-time Pro Bowler in six seasons with the Colts

- Only NFL player to pass for at least 3,000 yards in each of his first six seasons

- Selected as the Number 1 overall pick by the Colts in the 1998 NFL Draft

About Eli

Height: 6' 5"   **Weight:** 218 lbs.

Birth Date: January 3, 1981

Birthplace: New Orleans, Louisiana

Team/Position: New York Giants/Quarterback

Accomplishments:

● Selected as the Number 1 overall pick by the San Diego Chargers in the 2004 NFL Draft (later traded to the New York Giants)

● Set or tied 47 records in four seasons at Mississippi, including most passing yards (10,119) and most touchdown passes (81)

About Archie

Height: 6' 3"   **Weight:** 212 lbs.

Birth Date: May 19, 1949

Birthplace: Cleveland, Mississippi

Teams/Position: New Orleans Saints, Houston Oilers, Minnesota Vikings/Quarterback

Accomplishments:

● Two-time Pro Bowler (1978, 1979)

● Selected as the Number 2 overall pick by the New Orleans Saints in the 1971 NFL Draft

● Elected to the College Football Hall of Fame in 1989

MANNY MILLAN/SPORTS ILLUSTRATED

Archie
MANNING

Generation
NEXT

Kellen WINSLOW II

A generation ago, Kellen Winslow of the San Diego Chargers redefined the tight end position. Now the Hall of Famer's son, Kellen Winslow II, is ready to do the same. The Cleveland Browns drafted him as the sixth overall pick in 2004.

Winslow II made a name for himself in three seasons at Miami (Florida) because of his quickness, agility, and ability to gain extra yardage after taking a hit. As a sophomore in 2002, he led the team in receptions (57), was second in receiving yards (726), and scored eight touchdowns. In the 2003 Fiesta Bowl, he caught 11 passes for 122 yards, including a seven-yard touchdown that put Miami ahead in the first overtime period. (Miami lost to Ohio State, 31–24, in double overtime.)

During the 2003 season, Winslow II grabbed 60 passes for 605 yards. He won the John Mackey Award, which is given to the nation's best college tight end.

Browns coach Butch Davis, who recruited Winslow II for Miami, can't wait to see his prize pick on an NFL field.

Neither can his dad. But Winslow expects to see a new and improved version of himself, not a clone. After all, his son is faster than he was. "If I was Kellen Winslow 1.0," he says, "he's Kellen Winslow 2.0."

About Kellen II

Height: 6' 4"   Weight: 243 lbs.

Birth Date: July 21, 1983

Birthplace: San Diego, California

Team/Position: Cleveland Browns/Tight End

Accomplishments:

- Selected sixth overall by the Cleveland Browns in the first round of the 2004 NFL Draft
- Won the 2003 John Mackey Award as the nation's best college tight end
- Selected to the 2003 AP All-America team

■ About Kellen

Height: 6′ 5″   **Weight:** 251 lbs.

Birth Date: November 5, 1957

Birthplace: St. Louis, Missouri

Team/Position: San Diego Chargers/Tight End

Accomplishments:

- Five-time Pro Bowler with the San Diego Chargers
- Caught 541 passes and scored 45 touchdowns in his nine-season career, including a career-high and NFL-best 89 passes in 1980 and an NFL-best 88 passes in 1981
- Inducted into the Pro Football Hall of Fame in 1995

HEINZ KLUETMEIER/SPORTS ILLUSTRATED

Kellen
WINSLOW

Generation
NEXT

Chris SIMMS

Quarterback Chris Simms played with such skill during his four-season Texas career (1999-02) that Longhorn fans always expected more from him — like the national championship. It didn't seem to matter that he led Texas to an 11–2 record in 2002, making him the only Texas QB to win 10 or more games in two straight seasons. Or that he finished his career with the second-most touchdown passes (58) or the fourth-most passing yards (7,097) in school history.

That type of pressure can crush a young player. But not Simms. He had seen his dad, Phil Simms, receive the same kind of treatment from New York Giants' fans.

Simms is confident he'll win fans over, just as his dad did in 1987, when he led the Giants to their first Super Bowl title. He was named the game's MVP and went on to become the greatest quarterback in Giant history.

The younger Simms has his work cut out for him. He didn't take a snap in 2003, his rookie season, and is the Bucs' number 3 quarterback for 2004. But Tampa Bay selected him in the third round of the 2003 NFL Draft because they are convinced he's their quarterback of the future. Simms inherited a lot from his dad, including a strong and accurate throwing arm, a cool head in the pocket, and an unbending toughness. The plan is for him to study under veteran QBs Brad Johnson and Brian Griese this season, then compete for the starter's job in 2005.

And after that? Win the Super Bowl, just like his dad did.

About Chris
Height: 6' 4" **Weight:** 220 lbs.
Birth Date: August 29, 1980
Birthplace: Ridgewood, New Jersey
Team/Position: Tampa Bay Buccaneers/Quarterback

Accomplishments:
- Selected by the Tampa Bay Buccaneers in the third round of the 2003 NFL Draft
- Second-most touchdown passes (58) and fourth-most passing yards (7,097) in Texas history
- Two-time semi-finalist (2001, 2002) for the Davey O'Brien Award, given to the nation's top college QB

■ About Phil
Height: 6' 3" **Weight:** 216 lbs.
Birth Date: November 3, 1954
Birthplace: Lebanon, Kentucky
Team/Position: New York Giants/Quarterback

Accomplishments:
- Named a Pro Bowler twice in 15 seasons with the New York Giants
- Named MVP of Super Bowl XXI after completing 22 of 25 passes for 268 yards and three touchdowns in the Giants' 39–20 win over the Denver Broncos
- 18th on the NFL all-time list for passing yards (33,462)
- Holds or shares 14 New York Giants' records

LOU CAPOZZOLA

Phil SIMMS

Brian GRIESE

Quarterback Brian Griese knows something about perfection. In 1997, he led the Michigan Wolverines to a 12–0 record and a 21–16 Rose Bowl victory over Washington State that gave the team a share of the national championship.

Griese's dad, Bob, was the Miami Dolphins' quarterback in 1972 when his team produced the only perfect season in NFL history: 17–0. That record included Super Bowl VII, in which the Dolphins defeated the Washington Redskins, 14–7.

Like his Hall of Fame father, Griese has become a fine NFL quarterback. The Denver Broncos picked him in the third round of the 1998 NFL Draft. He took over the QB spot in 1999, after John Elway retired.

In his first season as a starter, Griese had 3,032 passing yards and 14 touchdowns. In 2000, he had 2,688 passing yards and 19 TDs and led the Broncos to an 11–5 record and a playoff berth. He was ranked Number 1 in overall QB rating that season. In 2001, he threw for a career-best 23 touchdowns. The next season, he threw for a career-high 3,214 yards. The Dolphins signed him as a free agent in June 2003, but he started just five games as their backup QB.

Griese signed with the Tampa Bay Buccaneers in March 2004. Leading the Bucs to another Super Bowl championship (they won the title in 2003) would make Griese *perfectly* happy.

■ About Brian

Height: 6' 3"   Weight: 215 lbs.

Birth Date: March 18, 1975

Birthplace: Miami, Florida

Teams/Position: Denver Broncos, Miami Dolphins, Tampa Bay Buccaneers/Quarterback

Accomplishments:

- Ranked Number 1 in overall QB rating (102.9) in 2000
- 2001 Pro Bowler
- Passed for 12,576 yards in six NFL seasons, including more than 3,000 yards in a season twice
- Led Michigan to a 12–0 record and the co-national championship in 1997

■ **About Bob**

Height: 6' 1" **Weight:** 190 lbs.

Birth Date: February 3, 1945

Birthplace: Evansville, Indiana

Team/Position: Miami Dolphins/Quarterback

Accomplishments:

• Won the Super Bowl in 1973 and 1974

• Named NFL Player of the Year in 1971

• Selected to the Pro Bowl six times

• Passed for 25,092 yards in 14 NFL seasons

• Inducted into the Pro Football Hall of Fame in 1990

NEIL LEIFER/SPORTS ILLUSTRATED

Bob
GRIESE

Generation
NEXT

D.J. STRAWBERRY

Guard D.J. Strawberry was a little-known senior when his Mater Dei (California) High School basketball team faced LeBron James and St. Vincent-St. Mary High School in 2003. By the final buzzer, that had changed. Strawberry guarded James so tenaciously that James committed seven turnovers and was 0-for-9 from 3-point range. "[LeBron] knew my name by the end of the game," he says.

So did coach Gary Williams of Maryland, who kept an eye on Strawberry throughout the season and offered him a scholarship.

Strawberry grew up playing baseball, which is only natural. His dad, Darryl Strawberry, was a three-time World Series champion and eight-time All-Star in the 1980's and 1990's. D.J. began focusing on hoops in high school because as a baseball player he was always known as Darryl's kid. As a basketball player, he could be just D.J.

Strawberry averaged 13.1 points and 4.4 rebounds per game as a senior at Mater Dei and led the team to a 35–2 record and a 2003 state division title. As a Maryland freshman, he quickly earned playing time with his hard-nosed defense. He averaged 6.3 points per game and helped the Terps reach the second round of the 2003-04 men's NCAA tournament.

■ About D.J.

Height: 6' 5"　Weight: 183 lbs.

Birth Date: June 15, 1985

Birthplace: Pasadena, California

Team/Position: Maryland/Guard

Accomplishments:

- Scored 6.3 points per game in 2003-04 as a Maryland freshman

- Named ACC Rookie of the Week after racking up 5 points, 4 rebounds, 2 assists, 2 steals, and 1 blocked shot against Number 1-ranked Florida on December 10, 2003, and a career-high 17 points against Pepperdine on December 14

- Had 13.1 points and 4.4 rebounds per game while leading Mater Dei (California) High School to the 2003 California Interscholastic Federation (CIF) championship

PHOTOGRAPH BY MITCHELL LAYTON

■ About Darryl

Height: 6' 6" **Weight:** 215 lbs.

Birth Date: March 12, 1962

Birthplace: Los Angeles, California

Teams/Position: New York Mets, Los Angeles Dodgers, San Francisco Giants, New York Yankees/Rightfield

Accomplishments:

- ■ 1983 National League Rookie of the Year
- ● 1988 National League home-run champ (39)
- ●Eight-time National League All-Star
- ●Three-time World Series champion: Mets (1986), Yankees (1996, 1999)

BRYAN YABLONSKY/SPORTSCHROME

Darryl
STRAWBERRY

Generation
NEXT

Luke and Chris
WALTON

As a rookie forward on the star-studded Los Angeles Lakers, Luke Walton was a bench warmer for the 2003-04 NBA season — until Game 2 of the Finals. The Lakers were floundering against the Detroit Pistons and in desperate need of a spark. Enter Walton. He raced onto the court and helped the Lakers defeat Detroit, 99–91, in overtime with 7 points, 5 rebounds, and 8 assists. (It was the Lakers' only victory in the series.)

"It amazes me how he can give me the ball," former Laker center Shaquille O'Neal said afterward, "and guys who have been playing with me for four, five, six years can't give me the ball."

That kind of court savvy runs in the family. Walton's dad, Hall of Fame center Bill Walton, was one of the best-passing big men in NBA history.

Luke blossomed as a player at Arizona in his junior year (2001-02), when he had 15.7 points, 7.3 boards, and 6.3 assists per game. As a senior, he earned honorable mention as a 2003 All-America. The Lakers selected him Number 32 overall in the second round of the 2003 NBA Draft.

Younger brother Chris, a senior forward at San Diego State, is blossoming as well. As a junior, he averaged 8.7 points per game. In 2004-05, the Aztec offense will run through him and his numbers will probably spike even higher. Like Luke and their dad, Chris throws pin-point passes and plays with an intelligence that brings out the best in his teammates.

If both Waltons are playing in the NBA in 2005-06, it may be tough to tell them apart on the court.

■ About Luke

Height: 6' 8"   Weight: 235 lbs.
Birth Date: March 28, 1980
Birthplace: San Diego, California
Team/Position: Los Angeles Lakers/Forward

Accomplishments:
- Had 7 points, 5 rebounds, and 8 assists off the bench against the Detroit Pistons in Game 2 of the 2003-04 NBA Finals
- Selected as the Number 32 overall pick by the Los Angeles Lakers in the second round of the 2003 NBA Draft
- Third player in Pac-10 Conference history to finish his college career with at least 1,000 points, 500 rebounds, and 500 assists

■ About Chris
Height: 6' 9" **Weight:** 230 lbs.
Birth Date: October 31, 1981
Birthplace: Palo Alto, California
Team/Position: San Diego State/Forward

Accomplishments:
● Scored 8.7 points and pulled down 4.9 rebounds per game as a junior, in 2003-04
● Selected to the 2000 All-San Diego County team after averaging 16.8 points and 9 rebounds as a senior at the University of San Diego High School

■ About Bill
Height: 6' 11" **Weight:** 235 lbs.
Birth Date: November 5, 1952
Birthplace: La Mesa, California
Teams/Position: Portland Trail Blazers, San Diego Clippers, Los Angeles Clippers, Boston Celtics/Center

Accomplishments:
● Two-time NBA champion, with the Portland Trail Blazers (1976-77) and Boston Celtics (1985-86)
● 1978 NBA Most Valuable Player
● Elected to the Basketball Hall of Fame in 1993
● Named one of the NBA's 50 greatest players
● Number 1 overall pick by the Portland Trail Blazers in the 1974 NBA Draft

JAMES DRAKE/SPORTS ILLUSTRATED

Bill WALTON

Generation NEXT

Cheryl
FORD

The similarities are unmistakable. Detroit Shock forward Cheryl Ford, the 2003 WNBA Rookie of the Year, attended Louisiana Tech. So did her dad, forward and two-time NBA MVP Karl "The Mailman" Malone of the Los Angeles Lakers.

Ford stands 6' 3" tall and is a ferocious rebounder who led all rookies in boards per game (10.4) in 2003. At the end of 2003-04, her 6' 9" dad had pulled down 14,968 rebounds (10.1 per game) in his 19-season career.

Ford is an offensive force (10.8 points per game in 2003). Malone is second on the NBA's all-time scoring list (36,928 points), behind Kareem Abdul-Jabbar (38,387).

But Ford doesn't want to be compared to her father. "I'm trying to make a name [on my own]," she says. She did that at Louisiana Tech, where she was the Western Athletic Conference Player of the Year twice (2002, 2003). As a senior in 2003, she had 12.9 rebounds per game, third-most in the nation.

Now, Ford has put herself and the Shock on the WNBA map. She helped lead Detroit from last place in 2002 (9–23) to first place in 2003 (25–9) and its first WNBA championship.

That accomplishment is where the similarities between father and daughter end. Winning his league's title is one thing her dad has yet to do.

■ About Cheryl

Height: 6' 3"   Weight: 215 lbs.

Birth Date: June 6, 1981

Birthplace: Homer, Louisiana

Team/Position: Detroit Shock/Forward

Accomplishments:

- WNBA Rookie of the Year and WNBA Champion in 2003

- One of three WNBA players to average a double-double per game (10.8 points and 10.4 rebounds) in 2003

- Only rookie selected to the 2003 WNBA All-Star Team

■ About Karl

Height: 6' 9"   **Weight:** 259 lbs.

Birth Date: July 24, 1963

Birthplace: Summerfield, Louisiana

Teams/Position: Utah Jazz, Los Angeles Lakers/Forward

Accomplishments:

- Named one of the NBA's 50 greatest players
- Second-leading scorer in NBA history (36,928 points)
- Two-time NBA MVP (1996-97, 1998-99)
- 14-time NBA All-Star
- Two-time Olympic gold medalist with the U.S. men's basketball team (1992, 1996)

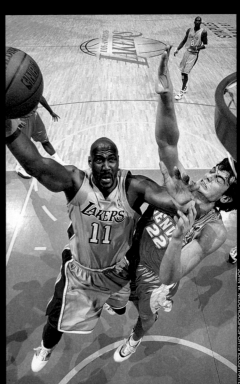

JOHN W. McDONOUGH/SPORTS ILLUSTRATED

Karl
MALONE

Generation
NEXT

EW

Patrick
ING, JR.

While center Patrick Ewing helped lead the U.S. "Dream Team" to the gold medal in basketball at the 1992 Summer Olympics, 8-year-old Patrick Ewing, Jr., was sitting in the stands, fiddling with his Game Boy. Eventually, he fell asleep. "I wanted to play," he remembers. "I didn't want to watch somebody else play."

Patrick Jr. — he goes by Pat — is on the court now. The slender, 6'8" forward averaged 2.8 points and 3.6 rebounds per game in nine starts as an Indiana freshman in 2003-04. He's an athletic player who likes to shoot from the outside or drive to the hoop. His dad had a low-post-playing, shot-blocking style. "He was seven-foot. I'm not," says Pat. "I can't do stuff like he could."

Ewing learned hoops playing many one-on-one games against his father. He caught the eye of college scouts in 2001-02, his junior year in high school, when he had 13.8 points and 8.5 rebounds per game and led Number 13-ranked Marietta (Georgia) High School to a 28–0 record. As a senior at National Christian (Maryland) Academy, he averaged 19 points and 12 rebounds.

When Ewing's famous dad isn't working as an assistant coach for the Houston Rockets, you'll find him in the stands at Indiana games — watching his son get it done.

■ About Pat

Height: 6'8"   **Weight:** 215 lbs.
Birth Date: May 20, 1984
Birthplace: Boston, Massachusetts
Team/Position: Indiana University/Forward

Accomplishments:

- Started nine games as a freshman for Indiana in 2003-04 and had 2.8 points and 3.6 rebounds per game
- Averaged 19 points and 12 rebounds as a senior at National Christian (Maryland) Academy in 2002-03

■ About Patrick

Height: 7'   **Weight:** 255 lbs.
Birth Date: August 5, 1962
Birthplace: Kingston, Jamaica
Teams/Position: New York Knicks, Seattle SuperSonics, Orlando Magic/Center

Accomplishments:

- Named an NBA All-Star 11 times and one of the Top 50 players in NBA history
- Scored 24,815 points during his 17-season career
- Selected by the Knicks as the Number 1 pick in the 1985 NBA Draft and named NBA Rookie of the Year in 1985-86
- Two-time Olympic gold medalist with the U.S. men's basketball team (1984, 1992)

JOHN W. McDONOUGH/SPORTS ILLUSTRATED

Patrick
EWING

Prince FIELDER

Prince Fielder is big. Six-feet, 260-pounds big. A born home-run hitter, his dad was saying on April 10, 2004. Prince had just stepped to the plate for the Huntsville (Alabama) Stars, the Milwaukee Brewers' Class AA team. His dad, former major leaguer Cecil Fielder, was a guest in the Stars' radio booth.

On the first pitch, *Boooom!* A monster homer, Fielder's second of the game. Up in the booth, his proud father smiled. Like father, like son.

Cecil knows a long-ball hitter when he sees one. He led the American League in homers twice (51 in 1990 and 44 in 1991) and the majors in RBIs for three straight seasons (1990-92). Through June 2004, Prince was tied for sixth in the Southern League in homers (13). During one week, he went deep in four straight games. Even with all that punch at the plate, "I don't consider myself a power hitter," says Prince.

The Brewers think otherwise. They were so convinced of Fielder's power, they offered him $2.4 million to sign in 2002. In 41 games that season, he hit .390, with 10 home runs, for their Ogden (Utah) Raptors Pioneer League team. Mid-season, he moved up to the Class A Beloit (Wisconsin) Snappers and batted .241, with three homers, in 32 games. The next season, he hit .313, with 27 home runs and 112 RBIs, with the Snappers.

If Fielder keeps swatting balls out of the park, he and his dad could become the greatest father-son home-run-hitting duo since Bobby and Barry Bonds.

■ About Cecil

Height: 6' 3"   **Weight:** 250 lbs.

Birth Date: September 21, 1963

Birthplace: Los Angeles, California

Teams/Position: Toronto Blue Jays, Detroit Tigers, New York Yankees, Anaheim Angels, Cleveland Indians/First Base, Designated Hitter

Accomplishments:

- Led the American League in homers in back-to-back seasons: 1990 (51) and 1991 (44)
- 319 career home runs, including 30 or more in a season six times
- Led the major leagues in RBIs three seasons in a row (1990-92)

CHUCK SOLOMON/SPORTS ILLUSTRATED

Cecil
FIELDER

■ About Prince

Height: 6'   **Weight:** 260 lbs.

Birth Date: May 9, 1984

Birthplace: Ontario, California

Team/Position: Huntsville Stars/First Base

Accomplishments:

- Named the 2003 Minor League Player of the Year by *USA TODAY*
- In 2003, batted .313, with 27 homers and 112 RBIs, for the Milwaukee Brewers' Class A Beloit (Wisconsin) Snappers
- Picked seventh overall by the Milwaukee Brewers in the first round of the 2002 major league draft

Generation
NEXT

Generation
NEXT

Sean
BURR

■ **About Jeff**

Height: 6' 1"   **Weight:** 200 lbs.
Birth Date: March 7, 1951
Birthplace: Long Beach, California
Teams/Position: Washington Senators, Texas Rangers, Atlanta Braves, Seattle Mariners, Oakland A's, Toronto Blue Jays/Rightfield

Accomplishments:

- Hit 240 home runs and drove in 882 runs in his 16-season career with five major league franchises
- 1974 American League MVP
- Hit more than 20 homers in five different seasons, including 41 in 1977
- Two-time All-Star (1974, 1978)

OUGHS
S

Star third baseman Sean Burroughs of the San Diego Padres has been making headlines since 1992, when he was 12. He led his Long Beach, California, team to its first Little League World Series championship that year. The team repeated as champs in 1993. Burroughs was named the tournament's MVP after batting .600 and pitching two 16-strikeout no-hitters.

One of Long Beach's coaches was Sean's dad, Jeff Burroughs, a 16-year major league vet who had 240 career home runs and was the American League's 1974 MVP. The younger Burroughs has the stuff to become an even better player than his dad. The Padres picked him ninth overall in the 1998 draft. In 1999, he hit a combined .363 for the Class A Fort Wayne (Indiana) Wizards and the Class A Rancho Cucamonga (California) Quakes, and was named the Padres' Minor League Player of the Year.

The next season, Burroughs batted .291 for the Class AA Mobile (Alabama) BayBears. He batted .322 with the Class AAA Portland (Oregon) Beavers in 2001. In 2002, he broke into the bigs and hit .271 for the Padres. He raised his average to .286, with seven homers and 58 RBIs, in 2003, his first full major league season.

Burroughs continues to make a name for himself. Through June 2004, he was batting .302 and the Padres were second in the National League West standings.

■ **About Sean**

Height: 6' 2"   Weight: 200 lbs.
Birth Date: September 12, 1980
Birthplace: Atlanta, Georgia
Team/Position: San Diego Padres/Third Base

Accomplishments:

- Hit .286, with 58 RBIs and 27 doubles, in 2003, his first full major league season
- Selected in the first round (ninth overall) by the San Diego Padres in the 1998 draft
- Played on the U.S. baseball team that won the gold medal at the 2000 Summer Olympics
- Led Long Beach, California, to the Little League World Series title in 1992 and 1993

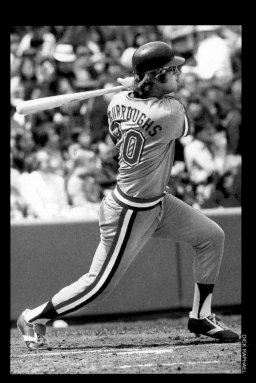

DICK RAPHAEL

Jeff
BURROUGHS

Generation
NEXT

Fernando VALENZUELA,

When most baseball fans hear the name *Fernando Valenzuela*, they think star *pitcher*, not star hitter. Fernando was a six-time All-Star with the Los Angeles Dodgers and one of the greatest pitchers of the 1980's. His son, Fernando Jr., is a clutch-hitting first baseman in the San Diego Padres' organization who is making his rep with his bat.

When he was in college — where aluminum bats are the norm — Fernando Jr. was itching to swing with wood. "If you have to use them in the majors, you might as well start using them in college," he says.

The slugger is well on the way to reaching his goal. He hit .390, with 20 home runs, in his two years at Glendale (California) Community College. Fernando Jr. transferred to Nevada-Las Vegas for his junior year. He hit .337, with 14 homers and 75 RBIs, and was named the 2003 Mountain West Conference Player of the Year. San Diego picked him in the 10th round of the 2003 draft.

He struggled a bit with their Class A Eugene (Oregon) Emeralds, batting .248, with five homers and 46 RBIs in 2003. But he has broken out in 2004. Through June 2004, he was hitting .307, with seven homers and 39 RBIs, for the Class A Fort Wayne (Indiana) Wizards.

Fernando Jr. has knocked in some big runs for the club this season. He won one game in the 12th inning with his fourth RBI of the night.

"Fernando's been pretty good in clutch situations," says Wizard manager Randy Ready. Sounds a lot like his superstar father, who was 5–1 on the mound in the post-season for the Dodgers.

■ About Fernando Jr.

Height: 5' 10"   Weight: 210 lbs.

Birth Date: September 30, 1982

Birthplace: San Pedro, California

Team/Position: Fort Wayne Wizards/First Base

Accomplishments:

- Selected by the San Diego Padres in the 10th round of the 2003 draft

- Hit .337, with 14 homers and 75 RBIs, at Nevada-Las Vegas in 2003

- Named the 2003 Mountain West Conference Player of the Year

JR.

■ About Fernando

Height: 5' 11" **Weight:** 195 lbs.

Birth Date: November 1, 1960

Birthplace: Navojoa, Mexico

Teams/Position: Los Angeles Dodgers, California Angels, Baltimore Orioles, Philadelphia Phillies, San Diego Padres, St. Louis Cardinals/Pitcher

Accomplishments:

- Named National League Rookie of the Year and won the National League Cy Young Award in 1981

- Six-time All-Star

- Led the N.L. in wins (21) in 1986

LENNY IGNELZI

Fernando VALENZUELA

Tony GWYNN, JR.

In his first college game for San Diego State, in 2001, Tony Gwynn, Jr., earned a good razzing from the fans after going 0-for-4. After all, his dad, Tony Sr., was a 15-time All-Star rightfielder with the San Diego Padres and one of the greatest hitters in baseball history.

Gwynn's coach, Jim Dietz, had also coached Tony's dad and he was worried that Tony Jr. was putting too much pressure on himself. After the game, Dietz encouraged him to carve out his own identity.

Starting then, and for the rest of his three-year career at San Diego State, Tony Jr. was called Anthony. With the pressure off, he began to hit more like his dad. In 2003, his final season, he batted .359, led the Mountain West Conference in stolen bases (25), and was named to the pre-season 2003 All-America team.

The centerfielder was drafted by the Milwaukee Brewers in 2003 and played for their Class A Beloit (Wisconsin) Snappers, batting .280 and stealing 14 bases in 16 attempts. He's now playing with the Brewers' Class AA Huntsville (Alabama) Stars. Eighty-one games into the 2004 season, Gwynn was batting .250 and leading the team in stolen bases (23). Now that he has confidence in his own career, he's no longer Anthony. He's back to calling himself Tony Jr.

About Tony Jr.

Height: 6'   **Weight:** 185 lbs.

Birth Date: October 4, 1982

Birthplace: Long Beach, California

Team/Position: Huntsville Stars/Centerfield

Accomplishments:

- Chosen 39th overall by Milwaukee in the second round of the 2003 draft
- Selected to the pre-season 2003 All-America team at San Diego State
- Career .341 batter at San Diego State

PHOTOGRAPH BY J2 PHOTOGRAPHIC

■ About Tony

Height: 5' 11"   **Weight:** 199 lbs.

Birth Date: May 9, 1960

Birthplace: Los Angeles, California

Team/Position: San Diego Padres/Rightfield

Accomplishments:

- Major league career batting average: .338 (17th all-time)

- Eight-time National League batting champion; batted .394 in 1994, the highest average since 1941, when Ted Williams batted .406

- Career hits: 3,141 (17th all-time)

- 15-time All-Star

- Five-time Gold Glove winner

RONALD C. MODRA

Tony GWYNN

Generation NEXT

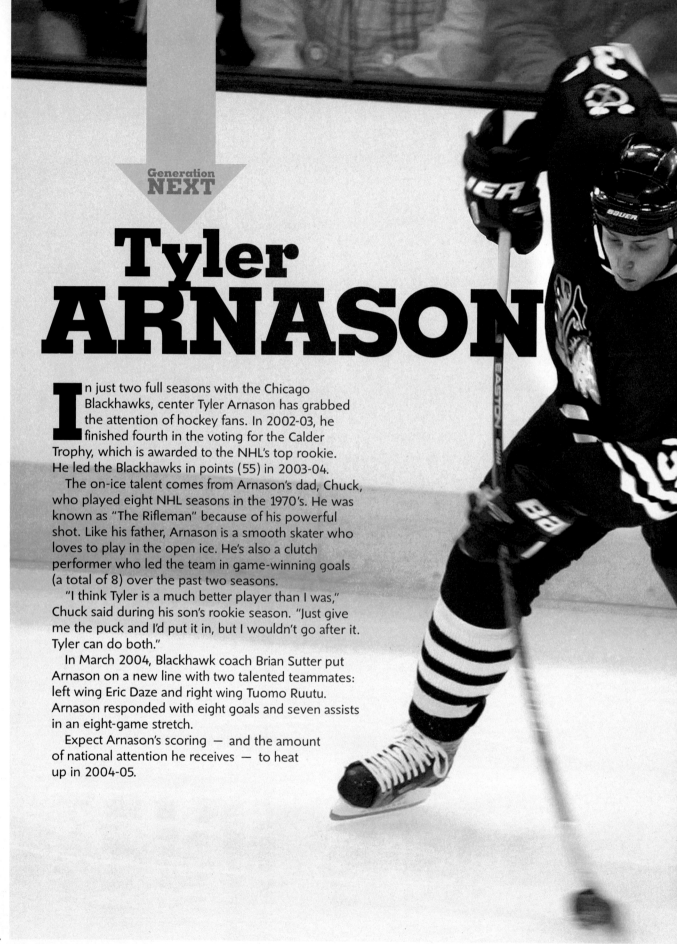

Tyler ARNASON

In just two full seasons with the Chicago Blackhawks, center Tyler Arnason has grabbed the attention of hockey fans. In 2002-03, he finished fourth in the voting for the Calder Trophy, which is awarded to the NHL's top rookie. He led the Blackhawks in points (55) in 2003-04.

The on-ice talent comes from Arnason's dad, Chuck, who played eight NHL seasons in the 1970's. He was known as "The Rifleman" because of his powerful shot. Like his father, Arnason is a smooth skater who loves to play in the open ice. He's also a clutch performer who led the team in game-winning goals (a total of 8) over the past two seasons.

"I think Tyler is a much better player than I was," Chuck said during his son's rookie season. "Just give me the puck and I'd put it in, but I wouldn't go after it. Tyler can do both."

In March 2004, Blackhawk coach Brian Sutter put Arnason on a new line with two talented teammates: left wing Eric Daze and right wing Tuomo Ruutu. Arnason responded with eight goals and seven assists in an eight-game stretch.

Expect Arnason's scoring — and the amount of national attention he receives — to heat up in 2004-05.

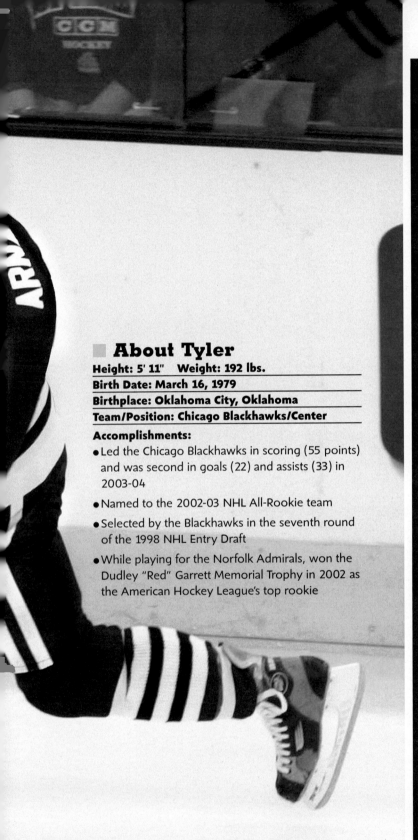

■ About Chuck

Height: 5' 10"   **Weight:** 183 lbs.

Birth Date: July 15, 1951

Birthplace: Ashern, Manitoba, Canada

Teams/Position: Montreal Canadiens, Atlanta Flames, Pittsburgh Penguins, Kansas City Scouts, Colorado Rockies, Cleveland Barons, Minnesota North Stars, Washington Capitals/Right Wing

Accomplishments:

- Scored 109 goals in eight NHL seasons
- Notched a career-high 26 goals and 32 assists for the Pittsburgh Penguins in 1974-75
- Chosen seventh overall in the 1971 NHL Amateur Draft by the Montreal Canadiens after scoring a league-high 79 goals for the Flin Flon Bombers of the Western Canadian Junior Hockey League

NEIL LEIFER/SPORTS ILLUSTRATED

■ About Tyler

Height: 5' 11"   **Weight:** 192 lbs.

Birth Date: March 16, 1979

Birthplace: Oklahoma City, Oklahoma

Team/Position: Chicago Blackhawks/Center

Accomplishments:

- Led the Chicago Blackhawks in scoring (55 points) and was second in goals (22) and assists (33) in 2003-04
- Named to the 2002-03 NHL All-Rookie team
- Selected by the Blackhawks in the seventh round of the 1998 NHL Entry Draft
- While playing for the Norfolk Admirals, won the Dudley "Red" Garrett Memorial Trophy in 2002 as the American Hockey League's top rookie

Chuck
ARNASON

Generation
NEXT

Generation
NEXT

Ryan MALONE

Right wing Ryan Malone got his NHL career off to a dazzling start in 2003-04. He finished the season leading the Pittsburgh Penguins in goals (22) and was the first NHL rookie to score three overtime goals since 1983-84.

Malone's early success didn't faze him. "I'm getting a lot of chances, and I wish that I could say I'm surprised," he told the Associated Press in November 2003. "But I've kind of expected what I've done so far."

Malone's dad, Greg, wasn't surprised either. Greg Malone was the star center for the Penguins from 1976-77 through 1982-83 and is now the team's head scout. One prospect he was sure of was his son, and he's glad the Penguins got him.

"With the way he has developed and come around, we all would have been upset if he'd gotten away from us," he said during Ryan's rookie season.

Drafted by the Penguins in 1999, Malone played four years of hockey at St. Cloud State, in Minnesota, before turning pro. He finished his college career in the Top 5 of the school's all-time leading scorers (56 goals, 84 assists).

Malone has become a fan favorite at Mellon Arena and a bright spot for the Penguins. The franchise has struggled with sparse crowds recently and has been a no-show in the playoffs for the past three seasons.

Now that Malone has established himself as one of the NHL's rising stars, the hometown hero is determined to bring the fans back and give them something to cheer about.

■ About Ryan

Height: 6' 4"   **Weight:** 215 lbs.

Birth Date: December 1, 1979

Birthplace: Pittsburgh, Pennsylvania

Team/Position: Pittsburgh Penguins/Right Wing

Accomplishments:

- First NHL player born and raised in Pittsburgh, Pennsylvania
  - Led the Penguins in goals (22) as a rookie, in 2003-04
  - Scored three goals in nine games to help the U.S. win the bronze medal at the 2004 hockey world championship
- Scored 56 goals in four years at Minnesota's St. Cloud State

■ About Greg

Height: 6'   **Weight:** 190 lbs.

Birth Date: March 8, 1956

Birthplace: Chatham, New Brunswick, Canada

Teams/Position: Pittsburgh Penguins, Hartford Whalers, Quebec Nordiques/Center

Accomplishments:

- Scored 191 goals in 11 NHL seasons
- Led the Penguins in goals (35) and points (65) in 1978-79
- Ranked 11th on the Penguins' all-time list in points (364) and 13th in goals (143)
- Selected by the Penguins in the second round of the 1976 NHL Amateur Draft

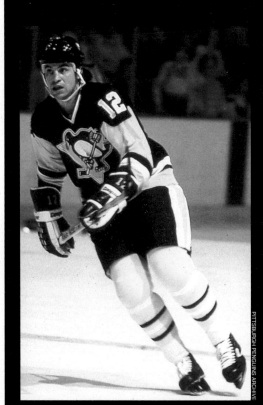

Greg MALONE

Generation
NEXT

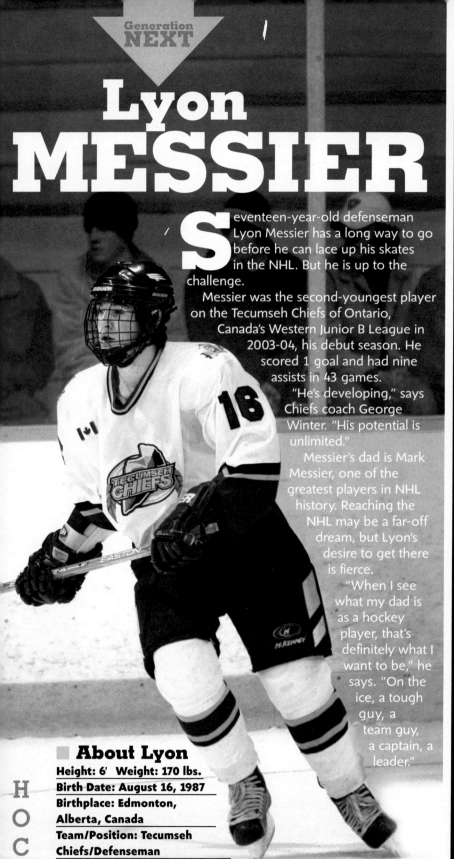

Lyon
MESSIER

Seventeen-year-old defenseman Lyon Messier has a long way to go before he can lace up his skates in the NHL. But he is up to the challenge.

Messier was the second-youngest player on the Tecumseh Chiefs of Ontario, Canada's Western Junior B League in 2003-04, his debut season. He scored 1 goal and had nine assists in 43 games.

"He's developing," says Chiefs coach George Winter. "His potential is unlimited."

Messier's dad is Mark Messier, one of the greatest players in NHL history. Reaching the NHL may be a far-off dream, but Lyon's desire to get there is fierce.

"When I see what my dad is as a hockey player, that's definitely what I want to be," he says. "On the ice, a tough guy, a team guy, a captain, a leader."

■ About Lyon
Height: 6' **Weight:** 170 lbs.
Birth Date: August 16, 1987
Birthplace: Edmonton, Alberta, Canada
Team/Position: Tecumseh Chiefs/Defenseman

Accomplishments:
- Scored 1 goal and had nine assists in 43 games for the Tecumseh Chiefs in the Western Junior B League in 2003-04
- Picked by the Junior A Sarnia Sting in the 15th round of the 2003 Ontario Hockey League draft

■ About Mark
Height: 6' 2" **Weight:** 211 lbs.
Birth Date: January 18, 1961
Birthplace: Edmonton, Alberta, Canada
Teams/Position: Edmonton Oilers, Vancouver Canucks, New York Rangers/Center

Accomplishments:
- 1,887 career points (second on the all-time list) in 25 NHL seasons
- Won the Stanley Cup six times
- Named an NHL All-Star 15 times
- Won the Hart Trophy as the NHL's regular-season MVP twice (1989-90, 1991-92)
- Won the Conn Smythe Trophy as the NHL playoff MVP in 1983-84

LOU CAPOZZOLA

Mark
MESSIER

H
O
C
K
E
Y

PHOTOGRAPH BY RICHARD OFNER